ELIZABETH AND PHILIP

Our Heiress and her Consort

ELIZABETH
AND
PHILIP

OUR HEIRESS AND HER CONSORT

An authentic sketch of H.R.H. the
Princess Elizabeth and Lieutenant
Philip Mountbatten, R.N.

by

LOUIS WULFF
M.V.O.

(Author of "Queen of To-morrow")

London
SAMPSON LOW, MARSTON & CO., LTD.

Contents

Acknowledgments

Thanks are due to P. K. Hodgson, C.M.G., C.V.O., O.B.E., for his courtesy in lending some pictures.

Acknowledgments are due to the following for their help in illustrating this book:

P.A. Reuters—Photos.   Photo Illustrations, Scotland.

The Scotsman.   Graphic Photo Union.

The Associated Press Ltd.   The Times.

The London Electrotype Agency Ltd.   Central Press Photos Ltd.

Fox Photos Ltd.

MADE AND PRINTED IN GREAT BRITAIN BY PURNELL AND SONS LTD.,
PAULTON (SOMERSET) AND LONDON

Author's Foreword

A FAMILY on the Throne, says Bagehot, is an interesting idea. It brings down the pride of sovereignty to the level of petty life.

In 1872, when the great constitutional authority wrote those words, the conception of Royalty was of something much more remote and aloof from everyday affairs than it is to-day when the British monarchy draws part of its greatest strength from its family associations. We speak of the British Commonwealth as a family of nations: and at its head there is a family on whom all eyes are turned as the proto-type and example of what family life should be. The foundations of the nation's glory are laid in the homes of the people, declared King George V; and turning his words slightly we may say with equal truth that the glory of the monarchy is in the home of the King. Nowhere was this more clearly demonstrated than in South Africa during the Royal tour. What impressed the home- and family-loving South Africans, especially those of Boer descent, most about their Royal visitors was the family party atmosphere of the Royal tour. Instead of a host of courtiers with high-sounding titles, the King and Queen brought their two daughters with them; and the Princesses went everywhere with their parents. That impression of the sovereign head of the Empire as the centre of a happy, united family did more than anything else to win the hearts of the Afrikaners, and so set the seal of success on the whole tour.

Now Princess Elizabeth is to be married with all the prospects of a happy family life of her own before her. The whole nation and the Empire at large join in wishing well to her and to Lieutenant Philip Mountbatten, the man of her choice.

Edinburgh and East Horsley,   L.W.
     July 1947.

Court Circular
Buckingham Palace July 9th

It is with the greatest pleasure that The King and Queen
announce the betrothal of their dearly beloved daughter
The Princess Elizabeth to Lieutenant Philip Mountbatten, R.N.,
son of the late Prince Andrew of Greece and Princess Andrew
(Princess Alice of Battenberg), to which union The King has
gladly given his consent.

How the news was given to the world

CHAPTER ONE

Royal Romance

IT WAS on the night of Wednesday, 9th July, that the Court Circular, issued from Buckingham Palace, contained this important passage:

"It is with the greatest pleasure that The King and Queen announce the betrothal of their dearly beloved daughter, The Princess Elizabeth, to Lieutenant Philip Mountbatten, R.N., son of the late Prince Andrew of Greece and Princess Andrew (Princess Alice of Battenberg), to which union The King has gladly given his consent."

The rest of the Court Circular that night was filled with an account of the reception by the King of four Indian Princes, the presentation of Letters of Credence by the new Siamese Ambassador, and the attendance of the Royal Family at the International Horse Show at the White City.

Simultaneously, the news was released in every capital of the Empire. It was flashed across the Atlantic, where it was "Page One" news from coast to coast in the United States. It was the official confirmation of news that the whole world had guessed was coming, and in newspaper offices, columns about the Princess and her fiancé, prepared long before, leaders on the Royal engagement, and agency photographs of the young couple, were rushed to the compositors to take the place of other news, hastily scrapped. The news "broke" at seven p.m., Double British Summer Time. But Fleet Street was not taken entirely unawares. There had, at the very last, been a "leak", and, as a result of a chance conversation in a bar at Athens, confirmed by a direct telephone call to Lieutenant Mountbatten, one London morning paper was able to state in its edition dated 9th July that the engagement would be officially announced "within two days". From Buckingham Palace, whence had previously come nothing but denials, there was now issued a statement that "The King has not yet authorised any statement about Princess Elizabeth. When he does so, it will be made through the usual channels." That was enough for Fleet Street. The engagement was "on" and that Wednesday was a day of intense activity, as reporters and photographers waited outside the Palace gates, followed the Royal Family party (without Philip) to the International Horse Show at White City, hurried down to Corsham, where Mountbatten was stationed, to interview any and every one who had anything to say about him.

Elaborate and strict precautions had been taken by the Palace authorities to prevent premature disclosure of the news in London. Only a very small number of Household officials were in the secret, and security measures went even as far as having the announcement typed separately from the rest of the Court Circular on plain paper instead of, as usual, on the official Palace paper headed with the Royal Crown. All these precautions, which succeeded completely as far as London was concerned, were taken not with a view to hiding anything from the public, but simply to make absolutely sure that this, the most important piece of "domestic" news since the Accession, should be given to the whole Empire at the same time.

A smiling greeting in South Africa

The Court Circular, issued daily from Buckingham Palace or wherever else the King and Queen are in official residence, is usually a somewhat dull record of the official activities of Their Majesties and the Princesses. It was made the vehicle for the engagement announcement because it is the only channel available to the Sovereign for communicating intelligence directly to his people: and the engagement of his daughter was a matter personal to the King, and not to be dealt with by such remote, impersonal and formal means as a message to the House of Commons, read by the Prime Minister. The Court Circular has, indeed, contained the announcements of every birth, engagement, marriage, and death in the British Royal Family for more than a hundred years.

That was the culmination of the engagement story.

Its beginnings go a long way back, to the days when Princess Elizabeth was little more than nineteen years of age. In September, 1945, a report emanating from Monarchist circles in Athens hinted that an alliance was contemplated between Elizabeth of England and Philip of Greece. At that time, it is certain that no engagement was planned. Speculation about whom Princess Elizabeth would marry was rife all over the world, in foreign capitals and the Chanceries of certain Embassies where a false political importance was attached to the affair, in the drawing-rooms of Mayfair, where elderly ladies consulted copies of the Almanach de Gotha, the record of European Royalty and nobility, to search out the non-Roman Catholic Princes of the right age who might be considered suitable suitors for the Princess's hand, and in London clubs and restaurants where members of the Princess's own circle of friends were to be met. All sorts of names were put forward, and it was enough for any eligible young men to be seen two or three times running in her company for another engagement rumour to be put into circulation, and often, on the other side of the Atlantic, where interest in the Princess is always intense, into print.

Very few people can point with any certainty to any one day and identify it as the day they fell in love. None of their friends, and probably neither the Princess nor Philip themselves, could determine when their friendship turned to affection and love. At the time when the rumours started, they had been friends for several years, and theirs was a growing and deepening friendship, which a frequent and uninterrupted correspondence throughout the war had done much to strengthen. When they first met is a little difficult to discover. Philip as a young boy spent a lot of his time at Brook House, the Mountbatten's home in Park Lane, and both Princess Elizabeth and Princess Margaret were frequent visitors there at parties given for the Mountbatten daughters, Patricia (now Lady Brabourne) and Pamela.

and the present writer,
one enquiry by radio to
was at Corsham, patier
his Princess should retu
African tour, the Princ
each other several times
one of the very first m
Philip, to which she re

That day was ano
and suggestions that
jack-in-the-box at th
published statement
her birthday. This a
last denial, as it turne

Back home from
Royal party left Wat
Palace, one Press pho
he declared, seen Lie
but had been unabl
Mountbatten" was
the King, who had

Lieutenant Phili
Family luncheon pa
eightieth birthday.
ment was settled in
pleasure to Her M
happy with the ma

From the Pala
rumours began to
ment which did no
between the coup
United States. It
Lieutenant had al
by reason of duti
as he had been th
But he was presen
Their Majesties g

It seems likely that the two must have met in those days, but Lieutenant Mountbatten's first recollection of meeting the girl who was to be his wife was at the Coronation of the King and Queen on 12th May, 1937, when he was a school-boy guest at the festivities.

There is no record that the two were drawn to each other on that occasion, and a long interval of two years and two months elapsed before they met again, this time at the Royal Naval College, Dartmouth, where Philip was enrolled as a cadet. After reviewing the Reserve Fleet in Weymouth Bay, the King and Queen, with their daughters, went on to Dartmouth, where the King had himself once been a cadet, and, after an inspection of the College and its inhabitants, took tea with the Commanding Officer, Captain F. H. G. Dalrymple-Hamilton. Cadet Prince Philip, as a distant relative of the Royal visitors, was selected to be present at the tea party. He and the Princess, not quite five years his junior, seemed to find

A family talk in Natal National Park

much to talk about, and it was Philip who proudly showed the Princess round the College, pointing out various treasures, explaining to her College customs. That evening, Philip, with a few other cadets, dined aboard the Royal Yacht. The war came, sending Princess Elizabeth to a long country sojourn first at Balmoral, then at Windsor, while Philip triumphantly finished his course at Dartmouth and emerged a fully-fledged midshipman, R.N., to be sent off to the Mediterranean. From his ship in the "Med." letters went to Balmoral, and from the Princess's wartime home answers went back. On leave in January, 1940, Prince Philip was entertained by the King and Queen, and went with them on a surprise visit to His Majesty's Theatre, where they saw a musical show, *Funny Side Up.* At that time, of course, Princess Elizabeth, not quite fourteen, was not considered old enough to go to theatre parties, and she remained at home at Windsor Castle, where the Royal sisters had been brought from Scotland for the first Christmas of the war.

Midshipman Philip went back to his ship, and did not see London again for many a long month. But the correspondence, we may be sure, continued, for Princess Elizabeth, like her great-great-grandmother, Queen Victoria, is a great letter-writer, and to have someone on active service as a correspondent was a matter of pride for any girl. When next home leave came round, Prince Philip was invited to stay at Windsor Castle. There, the two saw much of each other, and went long walks together in the Great Park. After that, Windsor Castle was open to Prince Philip whenever he had leave.

When Princess Elizabeth and Princess Margaret were producing their Christmas pantomime one year, Philip was a guest in the Castle, and, like everyone else, he was invited to see the show by the energetic and determined Royal producers. Since he had,

newspaper story, a fact
Foreign Office had take
about it. And, thirdly,
newspaper statement w
whether they would bec
This was very proper, fo
yet it was perfectly tru
standing there may ha
given his consent.

That winter, the P
at the weddings of frie
and parties. Earlier i
wedding of her Lady-i
Andrew Elphinstone,
with his cousin, the lat
setting of the ancient
of the Princess's was
Viscount and Visco
Brabourne, who had
bridesmaid, and this
the theatre—at the
where they saw *Perch*
her Prince were mo
squired Princess Eli
members of the part
present, driving the
sports car, the two
engagement grew s
moved to further de
Sir Alan Lascelles,
from the sea compl
who issued orders f

When Princess
pected to see Phili
But to the disappo
and Elizabeth had
Vanguard, the battl

Mountbatten wedding group: Left to right back row: Duchess of Kent, Viscount Mountbatten, H.M. the King, Viscountess Mountbatten, Squadron Leader Charles Harris St. John (best man): second row: Doreen, Lady Brabourne, Dowager Marchioness of Milford Haven, Lord Brabourne, the Hon. Patricia Mountbatten (bride and bridegroom), H.M. the Queen, Agatha, Marchioness of Sligo, the bridegroom's grandmother: front row: the Hon. Pamela Mountbatten, Princess Alexandra of Kent, Princess Margaret, Princess Elizabeth

of Windsor Castle a small party of about one hundred young folk, all of them close friends of the young pair, danced to music from a band which went on playing until well after three in the morning, and Princess Elizabeth and Philip missed scarcely one dance together. It was really a pre-engagement party, for the announcement came only a fortnight later. When she heard of the newest rumours, the Princess dismissed them, as she had the earlier ones of her premature engagement, with a smile, a smile that delighted senior members of the Royal Household, for it showed clearly that Princess Elizabeth has too strong a character to allow idle gossip or newspaper reports to affect her or to interfere with her happiness, a most valuable outlook for anyone whose life and actions are constantly in the public eye.

The best answer to the oft-repeated question whether this Royal romance between the Princess who is heiress to the greatest throne in the world and the Royal-born young man who threw away his titles and rank to become one of her father's subjects, is a

In "Service rig" at sea :
Princess Elizabeth wears a "Vanguard" ribbon

real love match or not, is to watch the Princess and Philip when they are dancing together. Each is a good dancer with any partner, but when they are dancing with each other there is something in the rhythm of their steps, something in the way they look at each other, that tells their story. They seem—and are—completely happy in each other's company. When they are not on the dance floor, when they are walking, not arm in arm, for that is something that Royalty does not do in public, but side by side at some official visit the Princess is making, it is easy to see their affection, which shows itself in a hundred different ways. During the Scottish tour, for instance, when Mountbatten first appeared in company with the Royal party, while the packed throngs were cheering the Royal visitors as they walked slowly round the crowded square of Kelso, there was one small person who was not enjoying it in the least, a baby in its mother's arms, crying with a passionate conviction that this Royal occasion was not in his line at all. Philip, noticing the unwilling spectator, drew Princess Elizabeth's attention to him, touching her arm and whispering a comment to her that brought a smile to her lips. Again, in the formality and dignity of the proceedings at Edinburgh's Usher Hall, where Lord Provost Sir John Falconer had just made the Princess a Free Burgess of the city, Mountbatten struck a charming human note. He watched closely as the Princess made her speech. When she finished and resumed her seat, at once her fiancé, forgetful that there was an attentive lady-in-waiting behind, leaned forward and put out his hands to relieve the Princess of her manuscript. At an Edinburgh Service Club, where the Princess was asked to sign the Visitors' Book, there was, by an oversight, no pen for her use. Immediately, Philip produced a fountain-pen from his pocket and handed it to her—receiving it back a few moments later to sign his own name for the first time underneath hers. Small incidents as these are, they show that spontaneous attentiveness that springs from true affection.

Dancing is but one of the many tastes the Princess and Philip share in common. Another is the theatre. Each is fond of seeing any piece of the theatre, from a serious play to a musical comedy, and Philip has, like the Princess, a love of music. He is not so good a pianist as she, and has not taken part in the madrigal singing by a choir of some thirty-three which the Princess arranges every Thursday evening at the Palace. Reading is another interest they have in common, and their literary tastes are much the same, though their serious reading has necessarily hitherto been on diverse lines, the Princess concentrating on such studies as the British constitution, and constitutional history, while Mountbatten has read naval strategy and history, the lives of famous naval commanders, the accounts of famous naval battles. But he has not confined his reading exclusively to Navy matters. Economics, modern European and world history, and the development of political and national movements have been among his special studies.

Another of the mutual interests that bind the two is a love of the outdoors. Princess Elizabeth is rarely happier than when she is walking or riding in the country, far away from crowds, and Lieutenant Mountbatten has all the sailor's traditional love for the green quiet of the English countryside.

One more story of their stay in Scotland shows that Lieutenant Mountbatten, like other young men in love, will do much for his lady. At the big dance at the Edinburgh Assembly Rooms on the night of their arrival, the first public dance they had attended together, the opening dance was, not unexpectedly, a double eightsome reel. Now, Princess Elizabeth is a real expert at the Scottish dances, which she first learned as a little girl at Balmoral from King George V's piper, Pipe Major Forsyth. Mountbatten is not. For the first dance, therefore, he stood at the side, watching the Princess partnered

A morning walk on Table Mountain

by a young Scotch expert. Two days later, there was another dance at the Assembly Rooms, this time the Highland Brigade Ball, organised by the six Highland Regiments. Again, the first dance was a reel, with six sets, one from each regiment. This time the Princess, dancing as Colonel-in-Chief of the Regiment, in the Argyll and Sutherland Highlanders set, was partnered by Lieutenant Mountbatten. And he scarcely put a foot wrong. With that thoroughness that is a family characteristic of the Mountbattens, he had spent all his spare time in the interval between the two dances taking lessons in the reel steps from Princess Elizabeth and from Pipe Major MacDonald, late of the Scots Guards, now Piper to the King.

Not very long ago, Royal marriages were arranged with or without the consent of the two people most immediately concerned, for "reasons of State". No such reasons lie behind Princess Elizabeth's choice of a husband. If there is one thing more certain than any other about this Royal match, it is that the Princess was allowed unfettered freedom to make her choice, without suggestions or prompting from the King or any of his Ministers. There is one reason and one reason only for the marriage of Elizabeth and Philip, and it is the best reason of all: they are in love.

H.R.H. Prince Philip :
a study taken before he relinquished his Greek titles

CHAPTER TWO

Philip the Fair

SINCE Princess Elizabeth was looked on, and rightly looked on, as the most eligible girl in the world, the amount of public interest in her was exceeded only, in the five years between her first emergence into public life at sixteen and her twenty-first birthday, by the focus of world curiosity about the man whom she would marry. And that curiosity, legitimate enough in view of the high and responsible part the consort of the Heiress to the Throne may at any time be called upon to shoulder, is still, to a very large extent, unsatisfied even to-day, when the name of Philip Mountbatten has been blazoned from one end of the earth to the other, when his smiling face with its strong mouth and determined chin are familiar to everyone from newspaper pictures and news reels. For Lieutenant Mountbatten shares with our own Royal Family, among many other qualities, that of disliking publicity about his private life and affairs, and until the day when his name appeared first in the Court Circular, on the night of Wednesday, July 9, 1947, he regarded himself as a private citizen, his business as concerning none but himself.

For this reason, there are few pictures current of the former Prince before he became affianced to his Princess: and few stories are known about him in his early days.

To-day he is proud of two things, of his war-won British nationality (for his naturalisation as a British subject on February 26, 1947, was in no way the result of Court influence or priority demands by the King, but was his due as a foreign national who had served throughout the war in the British forces) and of his service and rank in the Royal Navy. Indeed, one of the best ways of assessing the character and personality of the man who has won the heart and affections of Princess Elizabeth is to visualise the traditional officer of the Royal Navy, silent about his job, modest about his attainments, ready and competent to deal with any situation, however difficult and unexpected, whose popularity among his men is all the more valuable because it is so entirely unsought.

Philip Mountbatten has all these attributes, and many more. Never seeking popularity in any way, he has been a most popular figure with his equals, superiors and inferiors, wherever he has been: at his Scottish public school with the other boys and his masters, at Dartmouth with cadets and instructors alike, as "Jimmy the One", or First Lieutenant, of two destroyers in wartime, equally on the lower-deck and in the wardroom. This quality of gaining popular esteem and affection without striving, so valuable and indeed necessary to members of the Royal House in a constitutional monarchy, was most clearly shown during the Scottish visit which followed almost immediately after the announcement of his engagement to Princess Elizabeth. In many quarters, as the pre-engagement rumours grew in strength, there had been a certain amount of ill-based feeling expressed against the match because of Philip's foreign blood. In Scotland, where for many a long year there had been hopes that

more congenial atmosphere, and set up a small public school at Gordonstoun, near the Scottish fishing village of Hopeman in Morayshire, perched high on the cliffs over-looking the North Sea, and there Philip followed him. Even had Mr. Hahn remained in Germany, however, his princely pupil would have left his Salem school, for to the well-balanced mind of the youngster of twelve years, there was something irresistibly comic about the Nazi salute with which his fellow pupils and their seniors greeted each other. Despite several warnings, Philip refused to conceal his mirth, and since this attitude was not exactly likely to endear him or his family—one of his sisters had married the son of Prince Max of Baden—to the authorities, it was decided to withdraw him at once.

Mr. Hahn, naturalised an Englishman, had the support of such well-known figures as the late Lord Tweedsmuir, Mr. Claude Elliott, Headmaster of Eton, and Admiral Sir Herbert Richmond for his new school, at which one hundred and seventy-eight boys, all of them from families of good standing, were enrolled. Among this small community, Prince Philip soon became popular, and soon found himself enjoying his new life very much. Mathematics and geography, both vital subjects for a future naval officer, were his favourite studies, and like most boys, it was at the subjects he liked best that he showed most promise.

Prince Philip goes to bat: he was captain of school cricket

Besides normal athletics, the rare sport of javelin throwing was one of the exercises encouraged at this far from conventional school, and the boy whose ancestry was in Denmark, the home of javelin-throwing Vikings, showed, probably by mere coincidence, a natural aptitude for this, besides being an excellent runner and no mean performer at the high jump. In his last two years he developed into an all-round athlete, captaining the school at hockey and cricket, and finishing as head of the school, a position in which he first showed those qualities of leadership and sense of responsibility which stood him in such good stead later on in the Navy.

One experience he had as a schoolboy of fourteen and a half has been shared by few officers in the Royal Navy. For a day, he acted as assistant coastguard at Burghead.

At Gordonstoun, Philip was regarded with great favour both by Mr. Hahn and by the other masters. A certain bond of sympathy had already been set up between the banished schoolmaster and his pupil by their joint, though differently expressed, attitude to Hitler, and the older man's regard for his pupil was increased steadily as Philip began to show those virtues and qualities that are his to-day. He was keen,

*At school he took a very great interest in amateur dramatics : Prince Philip (on left) took a
minor part in " Macbeth"*

intelligent and willing to learn, except for some subjects, Greek among them, which he
privately thought were of little value to him. For he had already made up his mind
about his future career. His family on his mother's side had a naval tradition established by his grandfather, the first Marquis of Milford Haven, who, as Prince Louis
of Battenberg, was for so long First Sea Lord, and who did so much to ensure Britain's
readiness for the naval war of 1914–18. That tradition was being carried forward
with typical energy and enthusiasm by his uncle, then Lord Louis Mountbatten, and
young Philip determined to follow in their footsteps if he could. But even in those
early days he was showing signs of that sturdy independence of character that is one
of his great charms. Hearing of his naval aspirations, a certain Very Important
Person, on a visit to Gordonstoun, offered to do what he could to help him to enter
the Service by dropping a word in the ears of influential folk at the Admiralty. But
the young Prince refused the offer politely. "I'll get into the Navy on my own or not
at all," said he, and that has been his way ever since.

For a boy with naval aspirations, Gordonstoun had many advantages. The fisher-
folk of Hopeman knew the schoolboys well, for it is part of Mr. Hahn's educational
theory to encourage his pupils to take part in village life, and young Prince Philip
spent many happy hours out of the schoolroom, helping to scrape the bottoms of
fishing boats, varnishing spars and going for sails. He was an enthusiastic member of

Lieutenant Mountbatten takes a class: Petty Officers listen to a lecture on current affairs

the school's Seamanship Guild, learning the difficult art of controlling a cutter under sail or oars, and taking part in two ambitious deep sea expeditions, one to the Norwegian coast and the other a cruise off the west coast of Scotland.

There is no surer testing ground for character than a small boat on a sea cruise, and Philip proved his worth to such an extent that his tutor, Commander John Lewty, reported that he was "a very cheerful shipmate, very conscientious in the carrying out of both major and minor duties, thoroughly trustworthy and not afraid of dirty and arduous work".

But he was, and still is, a person who enjoys fun, and who does not believe that all life is to be taken with grim seriousness. Whatever escapades were on, Philip would be in with the other boys, were it tantalising a village shopkeeper by making squeaking noises with wet fingers on a plate-glass window, or playing truant to have an unofficial swim. He was, by deliberate family orders, treated just like the other boys, an arrangement that suited him very well, for he did not like the fuss some people tried to make of him because of his Royal rank. Once, it is recorded, tired of being asked for his autograph by complete strangers, he obligingly took away a book and signed it—"Baldwin of Bewdley". After schooldays, this dislike of overmuch Royal fuss remained with him up to the day when he dropped his Royal rank and titles on naturalisation, but to people who approached him the right way, he would respond immediately, and the most treasured possession of a waitress in a certain well-known hotel to-day is the signature Prince Philip readily put in her autograph book when, against the strict rules of the management, she asked him for it as she waited at table on him and a group of brother officers.

When the time came for him to enter the Royal Naval College at Dartmouth, his school report contained these sentences: "He is a born leader but he will need the exacting demands of a great service to do justice to himself. His best is outstanding." And Mr. Hahn, who forwarded that report, added privately that he regarded Philip as his best pupil, an opinion that was amply confirmed at Dartmouth where Philip was awarded both the King's Dirk as the best cadet of his term, and the Eardley-Howard-Crocket Prize as the best all-round cadet of the year. Both these early achievements showed that the young naval aspirant had already taken to heart the sage advice of his uncle to do everything with a will and to set out with the intention of winning. To win the King's Dirk, indeed, was for Philip something of a special achievement, for he was what is known at Dartmouth as a "Pub", that is a Special Entry Cadet, who has already received his preliminary education at a public school, as opposed to a "Dart" or a boy who entered the Royal Naval College direct from preparatory school, and the "Darts" have the advantage of a longer experience of naval ways. His career in the Navy after he left Dartmouth in 1940 bore out his early promise. As a sub-lieutenant, still pursuing his course of training, though he had already spent some time at sea in enemy waters, he gained four "firsts" and one "second" which gained him nine months' seniority out of a possible ten. Later still, as a full lieutenant, aged twenty-one and four months, he was appointed first lieutenant of the destroyer H.M.S. *Wallace*, the youngest officer in the Fleet to hold the post of executive officer in a ship of that size.

At the Methuen Arms: Lieutenant Mountbatten in the skittle alley

His first ship was the battleship *Ramillies*, which he joined as a midshipman with the Mediterranean Fleet, transferring to the cruiser *Kent* when *Ramillies* left the Med., and later to the *Shropshire*. In January, 1941, still a "snottie", he joined H.M.S. *Valiant*, and was one of the most popular members of the battleship's gunroom. What the other "snotties" particularly liked about their Royal messmate was his complete lack of "side" and his total disregard for his own Royal rank. Only once, according to his fellow midshipmen of those days, did he venture to use his rank for personal advantage. Rejoining his ship, he arrived aboard some three days after his fellows, and when an explanation was demanded by his senior officers, he blandly recounted that he had been detained in London owing to an urgent call to the Greek Embassy on business connected with the Greek Royal Family. Whether this explanation was accepted is not recorded, but the incident had no effect on the Prince's promotion.

He was gazetted sub-lieutenant on February 13th, 1942, and served aboard H.M.S. *Wallace*, a seventeen-year-old flotilla leader on the East Coast patrol, in that rank until he was promoted lieutenant in July, 1942, and posted as her second lieutenant.

But it was as a midshipman that Prince Philip fought his first and only major fleet action, at the Battle of Matapan. As midshipman in charge of a section of the searchlight control, he had one of the vital jobs in that swift deadly night action, when in the space of five minutes the British battleships *Valiant*, *Warspite* and *Barham* blew the Italian cruisers *Zara* and *Fiume* out of the water. For his coolness and efficiency as he held the enemy targets illuminated with *Valiant's* searchlights, he was mentioned in despatches by the C.-in-C., Admiral Sir Andrew (later Viscount) Cunningham. And, when the action was over, this was Prince Philip's description of the battle: "It was as near murder as anything could be in wartime. We just smashed the Italian cruisers. They burst into tremendous sheets of flame. I just hate to think how much worse it would have been for the Italian warships if we had met them by day instead of in a night action." Short as was that experience in time, it is not in minutes and hours that the depths of an experience can be assessed, and the Prince who sat drinking cocoa after the action, outwardly calm enough, inwardly as excited and elated as anyone on board, was a different, an older, and a wiser man than the Prince of half an hour earlier, before his ordeal by fire. Three months before, he had taken a few days leave, telling friends in London, "This is a dull war. There's no shooting."

After two years in the *Wallace*, during which he covered the Canadian landings in Sicily in her, he was given a new appointment, that of First Lieutenant of

Lieutenant Mountbatten inspecting divisions "aboard" H.M.S. King Arthur, *H.M. training establishment at Corsham*

H.M.S. *Whelp*, one of our latest destroyers, which was completed early in 1944. It was the kind of post coveted by all young lieutenants of the executive branch, and it went to Philip purely on his record for efficiency as officer responsible for discipline and internal organisation in the *Wallace*. A First Lieutenant can, from the ratings' point of view, make or mar a ship, and *Wallace* and *Whelp* were both among the happiest of ships, as anyone who served aboard either will agree. That state of affairs, so desirable in a captain's eyes, so important to the fighting efficiency of a warship, was in no small measure directly attributable to Lieutenant Prince Philip. It was partly this that his commanding officer had in mind when he described Prince Philip as the best second-in-command he had ever had.

Aboard H.M.S. *Whelp*, Prince Philip went East, with the British Pacific Fleet, under Admiral Lord Fraser: and his Supreme Commander was his always-admired Uncle Dickie—Admiral Mountbatten, then Allied Supreme Commander in South East Asia. But the hazards of war which threw the uncle and nephew together ruled that there should be no chance of Admiral Mountbatten mentioning his nephew in despatches, something that would have given him the very greatest pleasure, for the Japanese surrender followed quickly without any repetition of Matapan, and it was at the surrender of the Japanese Fleet in Tokyo Bay on September 2nd, 1945, that the two met for the first time for some years. It is fitting that this young man, destined to take his place in the history of the British Commonwealth, should have been present then, to see so dramatic a page of history in the writing.

Two other stories of Prince Philip's young days in the Navy are worth recording for the light they shed on his character. When he found himself at Melbourne in June, 1941, he was, like all other naval officers and ratings, made much of by the generous, open-hearted Australians. But Philip's personality has a way of impressing itself on all who meet him, and it was five years after this, when his name was already associated with that of Princess Elizabeth, that the crew of an aircraft bound from Australia to Britain noticed a twenty-five-pound fruit cake among the freight was addressed to "Lieutenant H.R.H. Prince Philip of Greece". His Melbourne friends had not forgotten him. The other story also comes from the Empire. Two R.N. midshipmen, off an armed merchant cruiser, had difficulty in manipulating their spoons and forks when they were being entertained ashore at Halifax, Nova Scotia. They explained their blisters were due to an unaccustomed spell as volunteer stokers, when the Chinese stokers went on strike. One of them was Prince Philip.

Long before he had even met Princess Elizabeth, Prince Philip had determined, like his uncle, on a naval career. When his engagement was announced, it was stated on the highest authority, that he intended to continue in the Service. That, without doubt, is his own wish. But, as in the case of Viscount Mountbatten, who had to leave his post as Admiral Commanding the Second Cruiser Squadron in April, 1947, when duty called him to Delhi as Viceroy, duty may take him away from his beloved navy, and it is difficult to see how the twin responsibilities of husband of the Heiress Presumptive and those of an ordinary serving naval officer could be reconciled. In the normal course, Lieutenant Mountbatten, with his first-class record and outstanding ability, could expect promotion as Lieutenant Commander in about three years' time: and then a further eight years would elapse before he received the third ring of a commander, for naval promotion is, to a large extent, governed by length of service in the various ranks. If he were to stay in the Navy, there is little doubt that he would achieve flag-rank, for, like his grandfather and uncle, he is undoubtedly the stuff of which Admirals are made. But the Navy's loss may be the Empire's gain.

Princess Elizabeth's first autograph : she gave copies of this portrait, taken when she was seven, to Indian Princes who were guests of the Duke and Duchess of York at 145 Piccadilly.

CHAPTER THREE

Marriage and the Constitution

THE ROMANCE and marriage of any Princess are matters of wide and compelling interest, for marriage is one of the great experiences open to all mankind, whereas Princesses are creatures apart, retaining, no matter what their age or looks, a certain attraction bequeathed them by the idealised Princesses of our fairy tales. When the Princess in question is twenty-one and decidedly attractive in her own right, without any need to go borrowing from fairyland, the interest is all the greater: and when the Princess is also the heiress to a vast empire, the future wearer of the world's mightiest crown, the person on whom are set the affections and hopes of five great nations, each of which will one day claim her as Queen, the interest becomes world-wide, and embraces students of politics and diplomats as well as ordinary romance-loving folk.

Princess Elizabeth's marriage is unquestionably a national, or rather an empire, event of the utmost importance. Though her husband can never ascend the British Throne, or even share it with his wife, the position of consort to the future Queen is one of such far-reaching influence and potentiality that it is right for the constitutional aspects of the marriage to be examined.

Since 1772, when the Royal Marriages Act was passed, in the sixteenth year of George III, the matrimonial plans of any member of the reigning house in the line of succession to the British throne have been recognised as a matter of national concern. If a sovereign, or a potential sovereign, makes a bad marriage, it contains within itself the possibility, if not the probability, of a national disaster, a condition which, true enough two hundred years ago, is doubly true to-day when it is on the person of the sovereign and the example of his or her home life that the very cohesion of the scattered Units of the British Commonwealth—as the former Dominions are now officially and cumbersomely known—depends. Contrary to general belief, the Royal Marriages Act, whose terms explicitly govern the whole of Princess Elizabeth's marriage, as they did that of her father, do not give control of Royal matches into the hands of Parliament. The Princess had not to seek the consent of either House before she became engaged to Lieutenant Mountbatten, nor had the King to go either to his "faithful Commons" or to the House of Lords for sanction for the match. It is on the King himself that the Act of George III lays the responsibility of deciding whether or not a suitor is a fit and proper person to marry into the line of succession. It was therefore the King's consent which was necessary before the Princess's engagement, let alone her marriage, could legally take place.

"No descendant of His late Majesty George II, male or female (other than the issue of Princesses who have married or who may marry into foreign families), shall be capable of contracting matrimony without the previous consent of His Majesty, his heirs and successors, signified under the Great Seal," is the significant wording of the Act.

Actually, Princess Elizabeth's engagement was announced officially three weeks before the special meeting of the Privy Council at which the King made the declaration of his "consent to the contracting of matrimony". This is in accordance with long established custom whereby the Sovereign first gives his private consent as a parent,

Where she came of age: the Princess walks with her family in the colourful gardens of Government House, Cape Town

but announces it publicly in his Court Circular, and later gives his official and formal consent to the union "in Council".

Should the Sovereign refuse his consent, and the intending Royal bride or bridegroom being aged over twenty-five persist in marrying, the old Act provides a loophole, allowing the marriage to be solemnised provided twelve months' notice be given to the Privy Council—unless both Houses of Parliament declare their disapproval. No such question, of course, arose in the case of Princess Elizabeth and Philip.

Some misapprehension exists, particularly in the Dominions, about the reason for and the purpose of this pre-marriage Council. Strictly speaking, it is a legal, and not a constitutional, step, though the exact borderline between the law and the constitution is so vague and shadowy that not even the greatest experts can always agree on its precise definition. The King's declaration in Council is, in effect, the reading of banns for the marriage of a member of the Royal Family, and the fact that Princess Elizabeth happens to be heiress to the throne had little to do with the necessity for the holding of a Council before she could legally marry. The same procedure applies in the case of even the remotest descendants of George II, and there have been, within recent years, two or three cases of foreign princelings, descended from him, who have written to the King asking his consent to their marriages, though they were so far removed from the present Royal Family that the King had never met them. The Council which the King held at Buckingham Palace on Thursday, July 31, 1947, was not, therefore, for the purpose of giving assent to the intended marriage of the Heiress to the Throne, but to allow the King to declare—by reading aloud from a parchment scroll—his consent to the petition to marry put to him by one member of his House, in this case his elder daughter.

The presence of the four Empire representatives, Mr. C. D. Howe, Minister of Reconstruction and Supply in the Canadian Government, Mr. J. A. Beasley, High Commissioner for Australia, Mr. W. J. Jordan, High Commissioner for New Zealand, and Mr. J. Stratford, former Chief Justice of the Union of South Africa, was not constitutionally necessary, for the ordinary quorum of four members of the Privy Council would have sufficed. But King George V, with one of those happy inspirations of monarchy which were part of his strength, called Empire representatives to the Privy Council at which he consented to the marriage of the late Duke of Kent, the first Royal marriage to follow the passing of the Statute of Westminster, remarking that it would be much better and more fitting to make the marriage Council an "Empire family party". Since then, that precedent has been followed.

Princess Elizabeth was not present at the Privy Council meeting which determined her future: nor had she the right to be, for up to now, she has not been "admitted"—members of the Royal Family are not sworn in like other Counsellors—to her father's Council.

After the Council, two more steps were necessary before the constitutional and legal formalities were complete, the affixing of the Great Seal to the instrument setting forth the King's consent to "the contracting of matrimony between her Royal Highness Elizabeth Alexandra Mary and Lieutenant Philip Mountbatten, R.N., son of the late Prince Andrew of Greece and Princess Andrew (Princess Alice of Battenberg);" and the preparation by the Archbishop of Canterbury, on a warrant from the King, of the special licence for a Royal marriage.

Another and equally important Act controlling all marriages within the British Royal Family is the "Bill of Rights", passed in the first year of the reign of William and Mary, when England was still settling down after the religious troubles that were a legacy of the Revolution. The act for Declaring the Rights and Liberties of the Subject, and Settling the Succession of the Crown (1 W & M, C2.) expressly bars succession to the Crown from all persons holding communion with the Church of Rome, or marrying "a Papist". Should any member of the Royal House persist in an alliance with such a person, the Act rules that the people are absolved of their allegiance and the Crown descends "to such person or persons being Protestant as should have inherited and enjoyed the same, in case the said person or persons so reconciled, holding communion or professing (the Church of Rome) or marrying, as aforesaid, were naturally dead".

Princess Elizabeth watches native girl guides in Rhodesia

Philip takes the wheel; a royal drive without precedent

of his marked qualities, and again one of the utmost value in the crowded, sometimes repetitive life of constitutional royalty, is that of being interested in all he sees. To a Land Girl tending cattle, he will talk about butter-fat content, and other farming mysteries, to a cameraman filming the Royal party he will talk about lenses and exposures, and to a local councillor he will talk of housing problems. Nor is he a man to be fobbed off with half answers. He has, again like his uncle, the gift of easily assimilating and long retaining knowledge on all manner of topics. A public pointer to this side of his character can be seen in his recent visits to the House of Commons. A naval officer gets but little opportunity for studying the workings of the British system of Government, save by reading books, and in the future it is obviously going to be of great importance for him to know a good deal about the way our Government functions under a constitutional monarchy. Whatever is necessary to know for any job he is called on to do, he will learn. That has always been his rule of life, and he is likely in future to be a familiar figure in the Distinguished Strangers Gallery or in the new special gallery to be built for Princess Elizabeth in the new House of Commons.

To be constantly exposed to public attention, to have hundreds of eyes turned on your every movement, to be filmed and photographed wherever you go, these are part of the everyday ritual of modern royalty. Even to those accustomed to it from birth, it must remain something of an ordeal, and to one suddenly put into the very centre of the limelight the ordeal is correspondingly greater. So the seven days he spent in Scotland after the engagement announcement, appearing for the first time as a member of the Royal party, were in the nature of a trial—and no easy trial—run

*The Royal pair go off for a walk in the grounds of
Buckingham Palace*

for Lieutenant Philip. He emerged from it with flying colours and a greatly enhanced popularity. "If he goes on like this, he'll become one of the most popular men in the country," said one shrewd observer, not given to easy praise, after spending the week following the Royal party.

What the cameramen think of public figures is often an accurate, though rarely made public, guide to their worth. The men with the Press cameras are used to seeing great figures on the world's stage in all sorts of circumstances, and their opinions are not without value. Nearly every photographer in Britain will agree, for example, that Her Majesty the Queen is the best of all "subjects", a view which in different words expressed the world's opinion of the Queen. After a week with Lieutenant Mountbatten, they marked him down as a friend, and that is high praise. For his part, Lieutenant Mountbatten derives—as does Princess Elizabeth—a certain mild amusement from watching the antics of some of the cameramen who contort themselves into extraordinary postures in attempts to get some different "angle" for their pictures. After watching an exhibition of this kind one day with the Princess, the Lieutenant surprised one photographer afterwards by going over and congratulating him. "Thank you, sir, but what for?" asked the recipient of the congratulations. "Because you are the only one who stands up straight and takes the photograph without a lot of contortions. We've been watching you," said Mountbatten.

Mountbatten had been under "ordeal by (camera) fire" before. In the days when his name was first linked with that of Princess Elizabeth, photographers, under instructions from their offices, chased him a good deal, but with scant success, for he did his best to elude them. Now with the photographers present officially, he gave them every chance. It was on the morning of the engagement announcement that he had his first official pictures taken with Princess Elizabeth, in the Bow Room at Buckingham Palace, that pleasant red-carpeted room with its long french windows opening on to the gardens in the semi-circle that gives the room its name. This is perhaps the most familiar of all the rooms at Buckingham Palace to the outside public, for it is through this apartment that the bulk of guests at the Royal garden parties pass on their way to the spacious lawns. Inside the room and out on the Palace terrace, the young couple sat and walked while one photographer and one newsreel man took their pictures for all the world to see. Neither the Princess nor her fiancé were made-up for the occasion, and as any film expert will tell you, to have yourself "shot" by a cine-camera without make-up is by no means the way to ensure that you will look your best on the screen: and the resultant film of the betrothed couple certainly did not flatter Mountbatten's looks.

So far, his voice has not been heard on the radio. When it is, the public will hear a deep, firm, pleasant voice, with a decided touch of authority in it, and no trace whatever of any foreign accent. There is, indeed, no reason at all why Mountbatten should have any accent, since English has been his natural tongue since his earliest years. He is a good impromptu speaker, with little nervousness in his manner. Just a few days before the engagement announcement, he went to the tercentenary celebrations of his old prep. school, Tabors, now moved from Cheam to Headley, in Berkshire. Called on to speak, he said, "I feel like a new boy again," but went on for some eight minutes without notes, striking just the right note when he said he was one of the generation whose parents had spent money on their education only for them to be "snapped up by the Services" during the past war. "We were just old enough to go out and be killed," said Mountbatten, who lost many of his own friends and schoolfellows in the war. "I am one of the lucky ones, but a lot will not be coming home again."

That was the only public speech he had made before the engagement. But he is or hesitation. Prince Philip himself had to declare he was of good character, had an adequate knowledge of the English language, was, to the best of his knowledge, financially solvent, and that, were his application granted, he would either continue in the service of the Crown, or reside in His Majesty's Dominions. All that cost him, as it costs all naturalised subjects, a total of £10 2s. 6d., a pound deposit to the Home Office when he made his application, a half-crown fee to the Commissioner of Oaths before whom he took his Oath of Allegiance, and a final fee of nine pounds to the Home Office when the application was granted.

It is interesting to note that Prince Albert was naturalised only a few days before his marriage to Queen Victoria: that his marriage was the specific and only reason for his naturalisation; and that he retained his princely title of Prince Albert of Saxe-Coburg-Gotha all his life.

It was in 1944, when the end of the war seemed in sight, that Prince Philip formally renounced in writing his claims in the line of succession to the Greek Throne, a step he had refrained from taking earlier, while Greece was under German and Italian domination, because, as he told friends, it would look like deserting in the hour of need. But he retained his Royal rank and style until the naturalisation was completed, when he became plain Philip Mountbatten, with his naval rank as a Lieutenant his only prefix and title, a state of affairs that gave rise to no little confusion and caused many a heated argument in the days immediately following his engagement to Princess Elizabeth, for many people, meeting him with the King and Queen and the Princesses, as a full member of the Royal party, addressed him with the "Sir" of Royalty or high rank. Others, conscious that he had relinquished Royal rank, yet chary of calling him "Lieutenant Mountbatten", avoided the issue altogether. The exact forms seem a little obscure, but it could well be argued that the prospective consort of a Princess of the Blood Royal is, by simple courtesy, and of respect for his bride-to-be, entitled to the "Sir" which only the most churlish would deny him.

Another point of confusion arose over the question whether to bow or not. There is no rule that commoners, unless they hold extremely high office, like the Speaker of the House of Commons, are entitled to a bow, yet it scarcely seemed right to the many hundreds who met Philip and shook hands with him on the Scottish visit, to bow or curtsy to the four other member of the party, and give him a mere handshake. Most people compromised with a quick nod of the head which might be regarded as a bow or not, as you wished, and Princess Margaret, whose sense of the comic is well developed, watched with considerable amusement the indecision of various folk as they left her with an obeisance and went on to meet Philip, whose place was next to her. Nor did Philip himself, quick to note the humour in any situation, fail to appreciate the joke.

Aboard ship, of course, there was no confusion. The Royal Navy is well-used to numbering Princes, both British and foreign, among its officers, and the Service rule is that it is naval rank that counts, so when Lieutenant Philip Mountbatten saluted Admiral Sir Neville Syfret, Commander-in-Chief of the Home Fleet, instead of waiting to return *his* salute, as did the King, he was merely doing exactly what Lieutenant Prince Philip would have done a few months earlier.

CHAPTER SIX

Princess Elizabeth To-day

PRINCESS ELIZABETH has developed greatly in the year of her majority. Before she went to South Africa, two and a half months before her twenty-first birthday, she was still a young girl on the threshold of womanhood, a girl who had already shown signs of an independent character, a strong will, and a penetrating intelligence, but a girl whose sequestered upbringing left her younger, in many ways, than most girls of her age. The crowded memorable experiences of the great ten-thousand-mile tour of the Union, the vast number of new people whom she met, many of them with outlooks differing greatly from her own, her contact for the first time with the proud and sturdy Afrikaaners, her meetings with the Bantu peoples whose chanted songs she so much admired, the inspiring sight of the wide and limitless horizons of Africa, as the White Train moved across the veldt, above all, perhaps, the new and stimulating vision of the Empire as a great whole which Field Marshal Smuts opened to her as they talked together, all these combined to give her more maturity, to give her, as they gave anyone privileged to share that Royal journey, a deeper, more personal understanding of the conception of the British Commonwealth, an understanding of incalculable value to one whose birth places her at the very centre of it.

When Princess Elizabeth, sitting alone in a not very ornately furnished room at Government House, Cape Town, broadcast to the Empire on her twenty-first birthday, on April 21, 1947, and dedicated her life to the service of the great Imperial family, she spoke from her heart.

"I declare," said the Princess in that firm clear voice that the world has come to know so well, "before you all that my whole life, whether it be long or short, shall be devoted to your service, and the service of our great Imperial family, to which we all belong, but I shall not have strength to carry out this resolution alone unless you join in it with me, as I now invite you to do."

With her exact knowledge and lively sense of history, the Princess recalled the vows taken in more knightly days, and recalled, too, the words of William Pitt. "Most of you have read in the history books the proud saying of William Pitt, that England had saved herself by her exertions and would save Europe by her example. But in our time we may say that the British Empire has saved the world first and now has to save itself after the battle is won. I think that is an even finer thing than was done in the days of Pitt, and it is for us who have grown up in these years of danger and glory to see that it is accomplished in the long years of peace that we all hope stretch ahead.

"There is a motto which has been borne by many of my ancestors, a noble motto —'I serve'.

"Those words were an inspiration to many bygone heirs to the throne when they made their knightly dedication as they came to manhood. I cannot do quite as they did, but through the inventions of science I can do what was not possible for any of them. I can make my dedication with a whole Empire listening. I should like to make that dedication now. It is very simple."

"When are you going to become engaged?" The Princess, who might well have been taken aback by this rather brutal and quite unexpected intrusion into her private affairs, realised at once that it was only ignorance of Royal ways which prompted the question. She smiled without the least trace of embarrassment, and answered quietly, "You'll have to wait and see." But the old man was not to be lightly put off. "Won't you have an announcement for us on your birthday?" he asked. Again the Princess smiled, and answered him in the same words as before. Then she turned and left him, for further questions would have amounted to something less than politeness. Those few who watched the incident gave her high praise for her manner of dealing with it. That same necessity for readiness in parrying awkward questions was demonstrated to Lieutenant Mountbatten five months later in Scotland, when a somewhat forceful lady, having been presented to him, immediately asked, "Are you going to get married soon?" Philip smiled, for the actual wedding date was not then settled, and muttered a non-committal reply, which the lady in question later interpreted to eager reporters as a declaration by Philip that the wedding would be on February 11th. Only when they found that date in 1948 would be Ash Wednesday, did the Pressmen realise something was amiss.

It was in Scotland that Princess Elizabeth, in one of the many speeches which she writes herself, revealed a side of her nature which is not generally suspected. She has a poetical mind, and, in a speech in which she declared her great affection for Scotland, she conjured up a vision of a wanderer in a far land, with the pitiless sun beating down, whose thoughts "stray to some well-loved loch with a breeze ruffling its waters, the white clouds sailing overhead, and a curlew crying just out of sight. In bitter weather, the cold seems less unkind as we see in our mind's eye the long

Another birthday present : a casket surmounted with a gold nugget given by the residents of Hartley, S. Rhodesia. The King and Queen examine the gift.

hillside shimmering in the hot sun, with nothing stirring save the bees". Then, when most of her hearers at the lunch tables in the Assembly Rooms, where the Lord Provost was entertaining her after she had received the Freedom of his City, were letting their own minds wander away into some fastness of the Highlands, the Princess showed how much she knows of the orator's art. "You have noticed too that in such dreams the breeze never changes to a cold wind and a driving rain. The bees are there—but never a midge," she said, and the grave dignitaries of Scotland and their ladies laughed long at this sudden descent from Parnassus to the realities of everyday life. Another indication of the Princess's love of poetry is to be found in the number of times quotations find their way into her public speeches. In her twenty-first birthday broadcast, for example, she quoted Rupert Brooke—"Now God be thanked Who has matched us with his hour," and a score of other examples could be added.

The Princess, incidentally, made that important broadcast twice. Once was on her birthday, at Cape Town. The other occasion was a week earlier, while the Royal party were enjoying their only real rest of the tour, amid the peace and natural grandeur of that lovely country that surrounds the Victoria Falls, in Rhodesia. There, the

The Royal couple dance extremely well together at a ball in Scotland

Princess sat in the open, reading her speech in the strong African sunlight, while cinema cameras whirled, camera shutters clicked, and microphones recorded her words. This advance filming and recording was done with a dual purpose. The radio beam from South Africa to London, which would carry the Princess's words on her birthday, is, for certain physical and technical reasons, not entirely reliable. It is liable to sudden and unpredictable breaks, which, should they occur in the midst of her speech, might mean that half the Empire or more might miss large sections of it. To guard against this, the B.B.C., with the sanction of the King and the willing co-operation of the Princess, decided to make a recording which could be flown back to London as a stand-by, for use if radio conditions were bad on the birthday night. If, at the same time, the films and photographs were taken, they, too, could be flown back to London in time for publication on the birthday, instead of a week later. This was done, which explains the slight discrepancy between the newspaper reports which told how the Princess broadcast from a room at Government House, and the pictures which showed her clearly in the open air. But the B.B.C. recordings did not have to be used. The still uncertain factors that govern radio communications were favourable on the night of April 21st, and to her own satisfaction it was the Princess's "live" voice—to use the expressive radio phrase—and not a recording which listeners all over the world heard on her birthday.

Fascinated yet horrified: the Royal visitors watch Johannes handling deadly snakes at Port Elizabeth

A morning canter with Princess Margaret: on the sands at Port Elizabeth

beside the Tha
signation of his
with the Royal
which she, who
years, gladly di
open-air cerem
the earlier freed

To deal with
to follow, it bec
important post
family connecti
Cynthia Colvill
Mary for more t
Mr. Churchill t
to return to the
will make furth

But, as they
and Lieutenant
no house in Lor
St. James's or K
modernised and
much labour ar
work. So it wa
that for the tin
the first prepara
the Lord Cham
pressed staff wer
and looking up
real business of
dispatching inv
them, two room
self-contained s
floor which Pri
had as her own
were being got r
That is all tha
prepare a Lor
Heiress of Engl
groom, a sad r
of the austerity
but at the sam
example of the
British Royal F
way the lives of
The simplicity
dozen rooms as
in, too, with the
cess Elizabeth a
are people who

Another story concerning the B.B.C. is worth recounting. On the evening of the day the Royal engagement had been made public, there was a big crowd waiting outside Buckingham Palace in the hope of seeing the betrothed couple. From time to time shouts of "We want Elizabeth, we want Philip" went up. On the steps of the Victoria Memorial a group of cameramen with long focus lenses waiting patiently. Earlier, in the rain of the afternoon, the Queen herself, thoughtful as always of others, had sent out a message telling them there would be no balcony appearances before dinner, and the photographers had gratefully retreated to shelter, to resume their vigil later. On a mobile broadcast van, a B.B.C. commentator kept vigil too, and when his cue came in the middle of the nine o'clock news, he went on the air with nothing to report except the presence of the crowds. While he was doing his best to fill in time, what he and the cameramen and the crowds had all been awaiting happened. The Palace windows were opened, and Princess Elizabeth and her fiancé stepped out onto the balcony, followed by the King and Queen and Princess Margaret. Cheers broke from the crowds, the camera shutters worked, and the B.B.C. man was exultant at the supremely lucky timing of his broadcast, so lucky that it seemed as if it must have been stage-managed. But it was neither luck nor stage-management which brought the Royal couple and the others so opportunely onto the balcony. Princess Elizabeth, listening to the nine o'clock news inside the Palace, heard the commentator filling in time, and knew that was the moment to go out. It was yet another example of her instinctive sense of what to do and the right time to do it.

Since her birthday, Princess Elizabeth has taken on many new duties and has had many new distinctions bestowed upon her. But she is constant to her original rule not to take on more official appointments than she can deal with adequately and properly, and it is only after the most careful consideration to ensure that she will have time to take personal interest in its activities that she consents to any of the many requests which reach her to associate herself with societies and institutions of all kinds. On her birthday, the King appointed her Colonel-in-Chief of the Argyll and Sutherland Highlanders, and of the 16th/5th Lancers.

61

With the
herself familia
the Grenadier
which she took
from the "Soc
own ancestor (
accepted a dip
Grand Masters
ful Company o
Master) and h:
Royal Society
Margaret were
certainly the la:
announcement
Jerusalem. She
hall on June 1
City is renowne
she is by birth
since her father

luxury. Mountbatten himself was well used to much less commodious quarters before his marriage. The hut in which he lived at Corsham, one of the group of temporary war-time structures built with little regard for comfort, was no different from those of his brother officers, nor was it more elaborately furnished: and before that he had the cramped quarters of a warship as his abiding place. For her country home, the King gave Princess Elizabeth Sunninghill Park near Ascot, but because of the labour and materials shortage only a few rooms were made ready for the royal couple. Unfortunately the house was gutted by fire some three months before the wedding.

From Buckingham Palace, the Royal couple may go far afield in the days that lie before them. If circumstances dictate that Lieutenant Mountbatten must relinquish his naval career, he is unlikely to be content to live a life of semi-retirement, merely escorting the Princess on her public visits. He has too dynamic a personality, too energetic a mind for that. From Australia, before the engagement, came a suggestion that the King should appoint Princess Elizabeth Governor-General of the great Commonwealth, and there is no constitutional reason why she, or possibly her husband, should not undertake that office in Australia or any other part of the Commonwealth. The whole Empire has been wanting to see Princess Elizabeth for a long time: and the desire is even greater now that the Princess is no longer alone. Princess Elizabeth herself has made no secret of her desire to see as many parts of the Empire of which she may one day be the head. "Before I am much older, I hope I shall come to know many of them," said the Princess, speaking of the homes of the Commonwealth that are to be found in every continent on the earth, and she has a way of making her hopes come true. Where she and her sailor husband may travel cannot be told. But it is certain that wherever they go they will be happy if they are together, for theirs is a true love match: and this small account of the lives of a real Princess of the twentieth century and her princely consort may fittingly end with the words that rounded off the fairy tales of Princesses of a younger day, that they "may live happily ever after".

The King